In praise of *Keeping the Faith:*

"This book is an excellent and unique resource for battered women and all who care about them. With a rare combination of empathy, understanding, compassion, psychological and theological insight, and solid grounding in Scripture, Marie Fortune provides straightforward answers to the anguished questioning of women who live in fear, pain, and confusion and who long to know if and how their Christian faith addresses the abusive situations in which they find themselves. The author's style is warm, personal, and engaging. Reading the book is like reading a letter from a dear friend who deeply cares. For countless women, this book will be received as a gift from God, bringing new hope and comfort and the assurance that God indeed 'lifts up those who are bowed down' and 'heals the brokenhearted and binds up their wounds.'"

Letha Dawson Scanzoni, coauthor of
All We're Meant to Be: Men, Women and Change

"[Marie's] deep experience in this field is offered with care and wisdom. While this book is specifically for abused women, clergy will be greatly helped in understanding the pain and hopelessness of many abused women. Clergy will also gain understanding why the church has contributed to an abused woman's burden."

Arthur O. Van Eck, National Council of Churches
Commission on Family Ministries
and Human Sexuality

"This book will serve as a guide for women who have felt themselves shut off from the efforts of the battered women's movement to reach out to women in a secular mode. It will help to allay their misgivings about struggling to free themselves of the violence of their partners, and give them permission to ask for, to demand, something better. A fine and noble effort."

P. Catlin Fulwood, former cochair, National
Coalition Against Domestic Violence, and
former director, Southern California Coalition
Against Domestic Violence

Keeping
the Faith

Keeping the Faith

Guidance for Christian Women Facing Abuse

Marie M. Fortune

HarperSanFrancisco
An Imprint of HarperCollinsPublishers

Acknowledgments appear on page 105.

HarperCollins Web Site:
http://www.harpercollins.com
HarperCollins®, 📖®, and HarperSanFrancisco™ are trademarks of HarperCollins Publishers Inc.

ISBN 0–06–251300–1

An Earlier Edition of This Book Was Catalogued
As Follows:
Fortune, Marie M.
  Keeping the faith.
  Bibliography: p.
  1. Church work with abused women. I. Title.
BV4445.5.F67 1987 261.8´344 86–46208
ISBN 0–06–250339–1

  06 07 ❖ BANTA 20 19 18 17 16

*To my mother and father, who
taught me that no woman
should ever have to tolerate abuse
at the hands of any man.*

Contents

Preface

I am a Christian pastor, and I have been faced with the problem of family violence throughout my ministry. One incident illustrates some of the things I have seen and heard. I had been leading a support group for Christian abused women for several months. The group was regularly attended by six women. Several had been out of abusive relationships for a year, several were now in the abused women's shelter, where I led the group, and several were still in the abusive relationship. During one session, a new group member shared with us that she had run from her home with her three-year-old child just the night before. She was staying at a friend's house temporarily. Unemployed, she was very anxious about how she would buy food for her child during the next few weeks.

The women in the group were very supportive of her decision to leave and very sympathetic to her plight. They had either been there or worried about being there themselves.

After the session, as we were leaving, one of the regular group members took the new member aside and handed her a wad of food stamps. She said, "You may need these," and then turned and left.

There was no fanfare, no desire for acknowledgment on her part, no expectation of repayment. It was an act of grace and charity that I have seldom seen equaled in any church, and it brought to mind the biblical wisdom that "as you do to the least of these, you do to me." I am certain that for the woman who gave up her food stamps, it was simply the thing for her to do. Both women returned to the group the next week.

The majority of women in the United States were raised in Christian homes or as adults have affiliated themselves with a Christian church. This is a sociological reality. Therefore, when a woman is battered by a member of her family, she will likely bring to that experience her background and values as a Christian woman. Also likely is that her experience of violence in her family will be not only a physical and emotional crisis but also a spiritual crisis. She will probably have many questions about her faith: What guidance does Scripture give her? What is God's will for her? How can she deal with this situation in her life as a Christian woman?

In the past ten years, I have talked with many Christian women who have been battered or abused in their families, both as children and as adults. I have talked with women in their parishes. I have talked with women who were residing in shelters. I have talked with women who were in hiding, seeking to change their identity in order to escape from their abuser. I have talked with women who have been ostracized by their churches and counseled by their pastors to go home and be a better Christian wife in order to stop their abuser's violence. I have also talked with women who have found caring and support from their pastor and congregation. I have led support groups for Christian abused women. I have heard Scripture distorted and misused to justify harm done to another person. I have prayed with women who needed reassurance of God's presence with them.

I have heard more questions than I ever imagined were possible about the Christian faith. And I have heard many answers. Through all these experiences as a pastor and educator, I have learned much from battered women who are also Christian. I have witnessed many instances of the power of faith to enable many women to no longer tolerate their abuse in the family. I have seen numerous instances of care and support extended by one woman to another. I have observed actions of enormous courage on the part of many women. In all of this, my faith has been strengthened by these women.

This book is a response to those questions, distortions, and misconceptions that I have heard, as well as a gathering of the Christian witness that I have seen in the lives of many battered women. It was written to enable more Christian abused women to keep the faith—with themselves and with their God.

The most significant contributors to this manuscript were the women whom I met in Christian Abused Women's Support Groups and whom I have counseled at shelters for abused women. In addition, I am indebted to many women in the battered women's movement and in the National Coalition Against Domestic Violence who have provided particular insights into the faith issues that confront so many battered women.

In addition, I am most grateful to Anne Ganley, Patricia Hunter, Ruth Ann Howell, Diana Lee, and Frances Wood for their responses to the material and to Frances Goldin for her persistence and support.

To You, the Woman

To You, the Woman

> Give ear to my prayer, O God; and hide not
> thyself from my supplication!
> Attend to me, and answer me; I am overcome
> by my trouble.
> I am distraught by the noise of the enemy,
> because of the oppression of the wicked: for
> they bring trouble upon me, and in anger
> they cherish enmity against me. (PS. 55:1–3)

The Psalmist knew what it was like to call out
to God for help in the midst of trouble. You have
known trouble; you have been the object of the
anger and abuse of another person; you may feel
overwhelmed by all you have experienced. And
when you call out to God, you may not be certain
that God hears your prayer. The Psalmist knew
these feelings, too.

> My heart is in anguish within me, the terrors of
> death have fallen upon me.

> Fear and trembling come upon me, and horror
> overwhelms me. (PS. 55:4–5)

You have known fear. You have lived with fear
each day. You have lived with the anxiety of never
knowing when your partner's violence may erupt
again. Perhaps you have feared for your life or the
lives of your children. The Psalmist also knew
this fear.

> And I say, "O that I had wings like a dove! I
> would fly away and be at rest.
> Yea, I would wander afar, I would lodge in the
> wilderness.
> I would haste to find me a shelter from the
> raging wind and tempest." (PS. 55:6–8)

Sometimes you may have thought, "If I only
had wings, I could fly away from all of this and
be safe." You may have longed for a safe place, a
shelter to protect you from the storm of abuse in
your family. The Psalmist also longed for this
shelter.

> It is not an enemy who taunts me—then I
> could bear it; it is not an adversary who deals
> insolently with me—then I could hide from
> him.

> But it is you, my equal, my companion, my
>   familiar friend.
> We used to hold sweet converse together;
>   within God's house we walked in fellowship.
> (PS. 55:12–14)

The person who has hurt you, the person whose violence you fear is someone very close to you. It is not a stranger walking down the street. It is a person you have loved and shared your life with. This makes the hurt much deeper. The Psalmist also knew the harm that came from someone very close and how much more painful that was than from a stranger.

You are a Christian woman, a woman of faith who has been abused by a member of your family. Your family may be traditional or nontraditional. Whatever form your family takes, you face all the problems of dealing with the abuse and its impact on you and your children. But you also face the possibility that your church does not understand or want to know about your experience as a battered woman. You may feel abandoned by your church; you may feel abandoned by God.

Now more than ever you need your faith and the support of the community of faith to be with you through this crisis. This book is for you. It is written to help answer some of the questions you may be asking as a Christian abused woman. It is written to help you understand some of the scriptural passages that speak to your situation but that may have been confusing to you. It is written to remind you that God is present to you even now and that there are Christians who do understand your pain, your fear, and your doubt. It is written so that we in the Christian community can keep the faith with you during this time of your life. We will not turn away from you; we will not abandon you. We will walk with you as you seek to end the abuse in your life.

This book is written primarily in a question-and-answer format. The questions are those that I have heard most often from Christian abused women. The answers are a beginning: they will help you begin to think in a new way about your situation and all the questions it raises. They are not intended to be the last word, but perhaps they will be the first word you have heard that makes sense in terms of what you know to be true in your life.

Following the questions and answers is a section of prayers, Scripture, and poems that is designed to help you with your prayer and meditation, followed by a section that can help you deal with your pastor, shelter counselor, and the other women you may meet in a shelter or support group. The last section is for clergy or laypersons who are seeking to help Christian abused women whom they care about. Finally, there is a list of readings you may want to turn to for further information and help.

❧ *Questions*
and Answers

Questions and Answers

Why Is This Happening to Me?

Your experience of abuse may be very new and unexpected, or you may have lived with it for many years. You may have heard many things from other people about why this is happening, or you may have heard nothing, since people don't often talk about this problem. You probably have questions about why you are being abused.

Maybe all those things he says about me are true. I probably don't deserve any better than I get. He's probably right.

Paul challenges us with this question:

Do you not know that you are God's temple and that God's Spirit dwells in you? If any one destroys God's temple, God will destroy him. For God's temple is holy, and that temple you are. (1 COR. 3:16–17)

You are valued in God's eyes; your whole self is regarded by God as a temple, a sacred place. Just as God does not want a temple defiled by violence, neither does God want you to be harmed. God's spirit dwells in you and makes you holy. You do deserve to live without fear and without abuse.

The one who destroys God's temple stands in judgment before God. God is displeased when anyone destroys what God regards as sacred. "That temple you are."

> *But my life has always been like this, hard from the very beginning. I watched my mother get beaten by my father. And my boyfriend has beaten me from the time I began to date him. This must be God's will for me. Shouldn't I just accept it and live with it?*

No. Just because much of your family experience has included abuse does not mean that God wants this for you. Jesus said:

> The thief comes only to steal and kill and destroy; I came that they may have life, and have it abundantly. (JOHN 10:10)

Here Jesus is saying that some people come among us to hurt and destroy others. Unfortunately, much of your life has been lived with such people. But Jesus brought something totally different from that. He came so that we might know fullness of life and feel safe and happy. Jesus refused to accept that the way things were in so many people's lives was the way they had to be. He wanted things to be different. When he promised abundant life, he was referring not to material abundance (cars, houses, boats, money, and so on) but to spiritual abundance. Primary to this spiritual abundance is feeling safe and unafraid in your own home, knowing that you are loved and respected for who you are. This is God's will for you and your children.

I am not a very good Christian. I have done some really bad things in my life. Maybe this abuse is God's way of punishing me.

There may be things in your past that you regret having done or that you are not particularly proud of. There may be sins of which you have not repented. You may not go to church regularly or do all the things that you think make a good Christian. But no matter what kinds of things you have done or neglected to do, you do not deserve to be abused, and God does not send this abuse to you as punishment. If there are things that you carry that you want to repent of, then talk to God about those things in prayer. But do not excuse your husband's abusive behavior by deciding that it is God's will for you. The battering is not God's fault; it is the responsibility of your husband. He has chosen to treat you this way; it is not God's will for you.

The Bible says that the wife must submit to her husband. Does this mean that I must submit to his abuse?

Actually, the scriptural passage that refers to the husband-wife relationship begins by saying:

Be subject to one another out of reverence for Christ. (EPH. 5:21)

This is the starting point for all our relationships as Christians, inside the family or outside. Here the words "be subject to" also mean "accommodate to" or "give way to." This means that we should all, including husbands and wives, seek to be flexible with each other and give way to each other. In another passage we find further clarification:

Let each of you look not only to his own interests, but also to the interests of others. (PHIL. 2:4)

So we are all, regardless of our relationship to each other, to be concerned for the other's welfare as well as for our own.

Then scripture proceeds to specific reference to husbands and wives:

> Wives, be subject to your husbands, as to the Lord. For the husband is the head of the wife as Christ is the head of the church, his body, and is himself its Savior. (EPH. 5:22–23)

This means that there are times in a Christian marriage when a wife should give way to her husband and recognize his interests as well as her own. But the husband's headship suggested here does not mean a role of unquestioned authority to which you are to be blindly obedient. What is described here is a model based on Christ's relationship to the church: Jesus was the servant of all who followed him, and he gave himself up for them. Never did he order people around, threaten, hit, or frighten them.

Almost all the rest of this passage from Ephesians spells out the instructions to the husband in his treatment of his wife: he is to be to her as Christ was to the church. This means he is to serve her needs and be willing to sacrifice himself for her if need be. This is what Jesus did for the church. He is to love his wife as himself, to nourish and cherish her. Another passage is even more specific:

> Husbands, love your wives, and do not be harsh with them. (COL. 3:19)

Clearly, the emphasis Scripture places on instructing husbands to care for and respect their wives just as Christ did the church leaves no room for excusing a husband's violent and abusive behavior toward his wife. Neither does your responsibility to accommodate to him and respect him mean that Jesus expects you to stay and tolerate his abuse. If he is not fulfilling his responsibility as a husband to you—that is, treating you with respect—you are not obligated to be a doormat for him. Your obligation is to provide for your safety and your children's safety.

> *Sometimes he makes me have sex with him when I don't want to. Sometimes he makes me do sexual things that I don't like. He says I have to; the Bible says it's my wifely duty. Do I have to?*

No, you do not have to submit to any sexual activity that you do not want. If a stranger forced you sexually, it would be rape. If your husband forces you sexually, it is also rape. His force may

take many different forms: he may talk you into
something he wants you to do, he may make fun
of you and call you a prude, he may show you
pictures and tell you he wants you to do this too,
he may threaten you, he may hold you down or
hit you. Just because he is your husband does not
mean you have to submit to his sexual interests.
Most states now have marital rape laws that give
you legal protection from this form of wife abuse
as well.

Scripture discusses sexual relationships between husband and wife this way:

> The husband should give to his wife her conju-
> gal rights, and likewise the wife to her husband.
> For the wife does not rule over her own body,
> but the husband does; likewise the husband
> does not rule over his own body, but the wife
> does. (1 COR. 7:3–4)

This clearly lays out the mutual rights and re-
sponsibilities for husband and wife in a sexual relationship, and they are exactly the same. Both
have a right to expect sexual activity with the
other, and both have a responsibility to respect
the wishes of the other. In no way does this Scripture justify a husband's forcing his wife sexually.
You have a right to say no to your husband's

sexual demands if you are uncomfortable, unin-
terested, or frightened.

Many women say that their husbands force
them to have sex immediately following a beating. Frequently the husbands say that this is because they love their wives and want to make up
after a fight. In fact, this forced sexual activity is
just another kind of battering.

Sexual sharing between two people is one of
God's greatest gifts to us. It is this gift that is cele-
brated in Scripture in the Song of Solomon (look
for this Scripture in the Old Testament). But
what is necessary for sexual sharing to be a blessing between two people is that both people be
fully consenting and that it take place in a context of respect, choice, and regard for each other's
well-being.

*My mother always said that if I made my bed
hard, I would have to lie in it. This one is pretty
hard, alright. Is this just my cross to bear?*

The suffering that you experience in being
battered physically and psychologically is suffering that is put upon you against your will. It is
involuntary suffering; you never chose it. It is the
same kind of suffering as discovering that one

has cancer because of exposure to a chemical dump or as the suffering of being injured by a drunk driver. You are harmed in some way because of someone else's negligence or cruelty—not because you choose to be harmed.

There is another kind of suffering. It is voluntary suffering. We freely submit to this kind of suffering in order to accomplish a greater good. We still do not like the pain involved, but we are willing to do it because we believe in something greater. For example, we are willing to undergo the pain of childbirth in order to bring a child into the world. We are willing to do without some material things in order to give money to our church or a program we support. In a larger sense, Martin Luther King, Jr., was willing to give up his life to help bring civil rights in our communities. This is voluntary suffering, and this is what is described in 1 Peter 3:13–17:

> Now who is there to harm you if you are zealous for what is right? But even if you do suffer for righteousness sake, you will be blessed. Have no fear of them, nor be troubled, but in your hearts reverence Christ as Lord. Always be prepared to make a defense to any one who calls

you to account for the hope that is in you, yet do it with gentleness and reverence; and keep your conscience clear, so that, when you are abused, those who revile your good behavior in Christ may be put to shame. For it is better to suffer for doing right, if that should be God's will, than for doing wrong.

What the writer is saying here is that when we stand up for what is right, as Martin Luther King, Jr., did, we will probably be reviled and abused— we will suffer—and that God will bless us because our suffering has a purpose.

But the suffering of being abused in one's family is very different. It has no good purpose. It never brings forth a greater good. It is not God's will for our lives. To accept it as purposeful, as your cross to bear, as God's will for you, is to allow yourself to be a victim. You do not deserve to suffer abuse at the hands of a member of your family.

When Jesus was crucified, he took upon himself all of our undeserved suffering. He did this so that we would not have to suffer as he did ever again. His resurrection is the promise that we should never have to tolerate such suffering in our lives again.

What Is Happening to Him?

Your husband or partner is someone you love, and there are times when he is loving with you and good to the children. But the other times when he is angry or violent, he scares you and the children. You have probably heard lots of excuses from him and from others for what he has done. Trying to understand him and what he is doing to your family can be very confusing.

Sometimes he is so nice and charming. He goes to church a lot, and everyone there thinks he is wonderful. They just don't know the side that I see at home. Which one is really him?

It is not uncommon for battered women to describe their partners in these terms. There does seem to be two sides to his behavior. His public image is often charming, wonderful, courteous, active at church or in the community; yet, your experience of him is very different. You see his abusive, angry, controlling, manipulative side at home. The Psalmist described this person:

My companion stretched out his hand against his friends, he violated his covenant.

His speech was smoother than butter, yet war
was in his heart; his words were softer than
oil, yet they were drawn swords. (PS. 55:20–21)

Do not deny your experience of his abusive
side just because no one else has seen it. God
knows what is in his heart just as you have experienced it. And that is what you have to deal with.

*Sometimes he beats the kids, too. He says they
need discipline. But I am afraid he is going to
hurt them.*

Unfortunately, the physical abuse of children
has been justified by some as Christian parenting. It is supported by misquoting Scripture, as in
"Spare the rod and spoil the child," which in fact
does not appear in Scripture at all. The verse that
has been distorted actually reads:

He who spares the rod hates his son, but he who
loves him is diligent to discipline him. (PROV.
13:24)

The point of this proverb is to encourage parents to discipline children—that is, to guide and
direct them. The rod was most frequently used
by the shepherd in biblical times to protect and
guide the sheep or to pull them out of dangerous

places, not to beat them; hence the reference in Psalm 23: "Thy rod and thy staff, they *comfort* me." Beating children with a rod is not what was envisioned as good parenting. Good parenting is accomplished by guiding, directing, teaching, and protecting children.

In addition, the writer of Ephesians cautions parents:

> Fathers, do not provoke your children to anger, but bring them up in the discipline and instruction of the Lord. (EPH. 6:4)

Since this verse follows the reiteration of the commandment to honor father and mother, the writer must be concerned about the misuse of that commandment in ways that cause harm to children. The caution is appropriate: nothing creates anger in children as quickly as abuse of them by parents. Anger at the injustice done to them is an appropriate response for an abused child. The writer places proper discipline in the context of gospel values: love, respect, care, and protection.

The caution is even clearer in Luke:

> It would be better for him if a millstone were hung round his neck and he were cast into the

sea, than that he should cause one of these little ones to [stumble]. (LUKE 17:2)

Children are vulnerable due to their age, size, naïveté, and dependence on adults. It is our task as Christians to protect them and to treat them with kindness and respect as we discipline them.

You need to take seriously your role as parent in protecting your children if they are being harmed by your husband. They cannot protect themselves. They are dependent on you. You are accountable to God for them. It is better to remove them from the abuse than to allow them to be harmed.

> *But he says that he has accepted Jesus Christ as his Lord and Savior, and he promises not to hit me anymore. I am so thankful that he has found Jesus; I feel like I have to go back to him now.*

If he has told you that he has been converted to Jesus, you should be somewhat cautious. If this is a true conversion, then he has only just begun on a very new road in his life. His conversion can be very helpful to him as he goes about the hard work of changing his abusive behavior and implementing his repentance for his battering. His faith can give him the strength to keep working on his problem even when he is discouraged. But he is fragile and needs guidance from a pastor who understands the task ahead of him and who understands his battering problem. His conversion is only the beginning, not the end. It does not mean that now everything will be fine or that now he does not need counseling to stop his abusing. If he thinks that his conversion is sufficient by itself, he is sadly mistaken. You should not be misled by this. In the Book of Acts, we read of Paul's purpose in his ministry—to insure that those who had not received God's word would

> repent and turn to God and perform deeds worthy of their repentance. (ACTS 26:20)

If your partner has truly repented and been converted, has genuinely turned to God, then he should perform acts worthy of his repentance. You should wait and watch for those acts; wait for him to no longer be abusive and controlling toward anyone.

If his conversion is not genuine, if he is only using this as a way to manipulate you or the legal system or his counselor, then you do not have any obligation to respond to him. In 2 Timothy, Paul warns us of such persons:

You must face the fact: the final age of this world is to be a time of troubles. [People] will love nothing but money and self; they will be arrogant, boastful, and abusive; with no respect for parents, no gratitude, no piety, no natural affection; they will be implacable in their hatreds, scandal-mongers, intemperate and fierce, strangers to all goodness, traitors, adventurers, swollen with self-importance. *They will be [those] who put pleasure in the place of God, [those] who preserve the outward form of religion, but are a standing denial of its reality. Keep clear of [people] like these.* (2 TIM. 3:1–5, New English Bible, emphasis added)

In other words, there are some persons who are abusive and hateful to others and yet who put on the facade of religion to cover up their true selves. God knows these persons and knows what is really in their hearts. God does not expect us to be gullible and to accept their religiosity at face value. If their actions in private are not consistent, if they are abusive at home but at church are zealous converts, then they are presenting the "outward form of religion" but are denying its reality. Their conversion is a fraud. Do not be deceived by it.

He needs me now more than ever. How can he change without me to help him? Shouldn't I stay and take care of him?

He needs help to change, but you cannot help him now. If he wants to stop his violent behavior, he needs to work with someone who understands his problem and will hold him accountable, someone who can teach him other ways to relate to people. He needs a counselor who specializes in working with battering men.

As long as you are there with him, you are an occasion for his sin. In other words, you are the one whom he feels safe abusing, and as long as you are there, he will abuse you; he will continue with this sinful behavior. This does not mean that you are responsible for his behavior; it is not your fault.

Leaving him temporarily and going to a shelter or staying with a friend will give him the message that you will not tolerate the abuse any longer. This can be of more help to him than anything else you do. He may finally understand that he is destroying what is most important to him. Your leaving may call him to repent more quickly than your staying and trying to take care of him.

I am afraid that my husband is also sexually abusing my children. But since he is the head of the household and I am under his authority, how can I challenge him?

Having authority in the family does not confer the right to abuse anyone. Authority is first and foremost a responsibility for the well-being of others. Whenever a person who has authority misuses that power to harm another, he then gives up his authority. When such a person becomes a tyrant, he should be prevented from harming others.

Jesus clearly reached out to children and regarded them as very special. The fact that he talked with them, blessed them, and lifted them up as special in God's eyes surprised and puzzled the adults who surrounded him. This was not the way that children were ordinarily treated. Jesus also pointed to our responsibility as adults to protect children:

> Whoever receives one such child in my name receives me; but whoever causes one of these little ones who believe in me to [stumble], it would be better for him to have a great millstone fastened round his neck and to be

drowned in the depth of the sea. . . . See that
you do not despise one of these little ones; for I
tell you that in heaven their angels always behold the face of my [Creator] who is in heaven.
(MATT. 18:5–6, 10)

Anyone who takes advantage of a child and
exploits that child is liable to have a millstone
hung round his neck. Any of us who do nothing
to stop the exploitation of a child are also responsible and may also end up with a millstone
hung round our necks.

What Can I Do?

Now that you recognize your situation as an
abused woman, what options present themselves? You are probably struggling to decide
what you should do in light of your faith: What is
God's will and direction for you now? You have
probably received a lot of conflicting advice from
people who care about you. So now you are con-
fused about what action you should take as a
Christian abused woman.

> *But Jesus said to turn the other cheek, to pray
> for my enemies, and to judge not. Isn't that*

what I should do now when he beats me or yells at me?

Jesus' teaching about love of one's neighbor is very clear. But he also presses us to love our enemies:

Love your enemies, do good to those who hate you, bless those who curse you, pray for those who abuse you. To him who strikes you on the cheek, offer the other also. (LUKE 6:27–29)

Does this passage mean that we are to simply allow ourselves to be beaten and abused? Does Jesus expect us to become doormats? Is this the "good" that we should do to that person who hates us?

In Paul's letter to the Romans, he discusses these ideas further and I think helps us to clarify the meaning:

Let love be genuine; hate what is evil, hold fast to what is good. . . . Bless those who persecute you; bless and do not curse them. . . . Repay no one evil for evil. . . . Beloved, never avenge yourselves, but leave it to the wrath of God; for it is written, "Vengeance is mine, I will repay, says the Lord." (ROM. 12:9, 14, 17, 19)

Jesus is trying to teach us that we should not act out of vengeance, that we should not seek to punish the one who harmed us by returning evil for evil. To turn the other cheek means that we do not return a blow for a blow. But we can walk away from it. He does not mean that we should lie down and allow someone to walk over us many times. There is nothing loving about allowing an abusive person to continue to destroy his family. Violence in the family is evil, and Paul clearly says that we should hate what is evil and try to bring it to an end.

Paul further clarifies the question of judgment:

> Therefore you have no excuse . . . whoever you are, when you judge another; for in passing judgment upon him you condemn yourself, because you, the judge, are doing the very same things. We know that the judgment of God rightly falls upon those who do such things. . . . For those who are factious and do not obey the truth, but obey wickedness, there will be wrath and fury. (ROM. 2:1–2, 8)

This does not mean that we should not judge. It means that a person who also beats his wife is not the one who can rightly judge your husband. But, clearly, God judges evil and calls persons to account for it. And we, too, as long as we are not engaged in the same behavior, can and should speak up and say no to abuse in the family.

Pray for the one who abuses you. Pray that he will repent and turn to God, that he will recognize the harm that he is doing, that he will seek help. But you need not stay there and be abused while you wait for him to hear God and repent. You can pray for him while you are safe in a shelter or safe home or living safely independently from him.

He is getting more and more violent. I am afraid of him and of what he may do the next time. But should I run away or stay and face it?

There are times when the wisest thing to do is to remove yourself from a dangerous situation if at all possible. The Psalmist knew this feeling:

My heart is in anguish within me, the terrors of
    death have fallen upon me.
Fear and trembling come upon me, and horror
    overwhelms me.
And I say, "O that I had wings like a dove!
    I would fly away and be at rest.

Yea, I would wander afar, I would lodge in the
wilderness.
I would haste to find me a shelter from the
raging wind and tempest." (PS. 55:4–8)

You should not have to live in fear in your
own house. You have the right to be safe. But it
takes courage to leave and to face the unknown.
Fortunately, now there are safe places for you and
your children to go. There are shelters and safe
homes or homes of friends where you can go.
This is only a temporary step, but it will give you
some time to think, to sort out your feelings, to
get some sleep, to make some decisions for you
and your children.

*I would like to talk with someone about my sit-
uation and maybe go somewhere safe for a
while. But I don't think those people at the shelter are Christians. I'm afraid that they may try
to take away my faith.*

When your house is on fire and you call the
fire fighters to come put out the fire, do you stop
and ask those people whether or not they are
Christians? God works in strange and mysterious
ways sometimes and may even send someone
who can help you who is not a Christian. You

may also find that some of the people you call on for help *are* Christians; they just do not wear a sign that says that they are.

The people who provide help for abused women through a variety of different programs are there because they care about you and do not want you to have to suffer any more abuse. They can provide what you need: a safe place, a time out, a chance to talk about what you feel and think, a chance for your children to feel safe, too, and information about the options you have. They will not try to force you to make any decisions. They will try to be understanding and sympathetic to all of your concerns, including your religious questions. If they do not feel capable of assisting you with these, they can help you to find a minister who can. Or if you want to go talk to your minister, they can go with you and give you support.

Do not miss an opportunity that God may have put before you just because it does not say "Christian" over the open door.

I don't want to go to that shelter. There probably won't be anyone there like me. Besides, if I go, I'll really be leaving my community. I'll be an outcast for sure.

You may be right; there may not be anyone there like you. But you may be surprised, too. Women of all ages, races, religious groups, and family styles are abused and go to shelters or safe homes.

And you are also right that you may have to seek shelter outside of your community. The advantage in this is that your abuser will have greater difficulty finding you than if you were to go to a neighbor or family member. But the disadvantage is that you will be in an unfamiliar setting and that members of your community may feel that you should not have talked with outsiders about what is happening to you.

This presents a very difficult choice for you: either you stay in your community and face the possibility that no one will help protect you from the abuse, or you leave to find a safe place but lose the support of your community.

Remember that Jesus always ministered to the outcast—those who, because of their particular circumstances at the time, were exiled from the community. Jesus will be present with you if you make the choice to seek safety outside your community.

More and more communities are developing shelter and support services for members of those communities. This is an important development that may mean that you can choose to stay or leave your community but still find safety and support.

> *When I married him, it was for better or for worse. This abuse is clearly the worst I can imagine. But doesn't the Bible say that I can never divorce him?*

Scripture does not simply prohibit divorce. Whenever it talks about divorce, it points to the importance of faithfulness to the marriage covenant and the protection of persons' well-being. In the Book of Malachi, one of the prophets, for example, we find this passage addressed to husbands:

> And this again you do. You cover the Lord's altar with tears, with weeping and groaning because [God] no longer regards the offering or accepts it with favor at your hand. You ask, "Why does [God] not?" Because the Lord was witness to the covenant between you and the wife of your youth, to whom you have been faithless, though she is your companion and your wife by covenant. Has not the one God made and sustained for us the spirit of life: And

what does [God] desire? Godly offspring. So
take heed to yourselves, and let none be faithless
to the wife of his youth. "For I hate divorce,"
says the Lord the God of Israel, "and covering
one's garment with violence," says the Lord of
hosts. "So take heed to yourselves and do not be
faithless." (MAL. 2:13–16)

Here the prophet is challenging the faithless-
ness of a husband. During that period, frequently
husbands would simply put out their wives
through divorce, and for no reason except that
they were tired of them. They had the right to divorce under the law, and they abused that right.
This is the practice that Malachi is challenging.

We have always taught within the Christian
tradition that the marriage covenant is broken by
adultery or sexual unfaithfulness in marriage. The
main reason that adultery is a problem is that it
results in broken trust between husband and wife.
If the promise is made to be monogamous, then
adultery breaks that promise. But we should also
realize that there are other kinds of unfaithfulness. Bringing violence into one's marriage is also
unfaithfulness. Once violence has entered a relationship, trust is destroyed. If you can't trust your
husband not to hit you, what can you trust?

When God says in this passage that God hates divorce, God is acknowledging the pain that we all feel when a situation reaches the point where a divorce is necessary, when the brokenness is so great that it cannot be repaired between two people. God does not say, "Thou shalt not divorce." But God grieves that unfaithfulness of any kind results in a divorce.

In Matthew, Jesus reiterates his concern for the misuse of the divorce proceedings for reasons other than unfaithfulness and says:

> What therefore God has joined together, let no man put asunder. (MATT. 19:6)

Any man who brings violence and abuse into his family life is putting asunder the marriage covenant that God has blessed. The violence is what breaks up the marriage, and the one responsible for that violence is the one responsible for the breakup. The actual divorce is in fact only the public acknowledgment of the private truth that a marriage has been long since destroyed by abuse. So if you consider whether or not to get a divorce, while it is a painful choice no matter what the circumstance, you are not taking steps to break up a marriage. Emotionally, that has already happened. You are taking steps to let other people know what has happened, to remove yourself and your children from a destructive situation, and to get on with your life.

This is not to say that reconciliation between you and your husband is not possible. Reconciliation is possible if he is willing to get help and stop his violent behavior. In this case, once you see real evidence over a long period of time of real change in him, of true repentance, then you may choose to consider a reconciliation. Or you may not. You may feel that the damage is too deep between you. In this case, you need not feel guilty for getting a divorce. But if you and he do seek to come back together, you will need to consider this a new covenant between you in which you are both really clear that there will be no violence under any circumstance. In this case, with God's help, your broken relationship may be healed.

But if I divorce him, doesn't the Bible say that I can't remarry?

Paul talks about marriage and divorce:

To the married I give charge, not I but the Lord, that the wife should not separate from her husband (but if she does, let her remain single or else be reconciled to her husband)—and that the husband should not divorce his wife. (1 COR. 7:10–11)

Paul here is referring to a wife leaving her husband for no good reason: if she does this, she must remain single in hopes of being reconciled to him in the future. This is a situation in which the marriage covenant is still intact. Paul is not talking about a situation in which a husband is beating his wife. This violence and immorality on his part have broken the marriage covenant. Not only can you separate and divorce, it is your duty to consider every option in order to protect your life and the lives of your children.

The purpose of Paul's teaching is to preserve a possibility of reconciliation within a marriage covenant and to prevent someone from going off and remarrying with no thought to the covenant they left. If you divorce because you are convinced that your partner is not repentant, then you are free from any previous obligation to that marriage covenant. You are free to remarry, and you will not be guilty of adultery.

Later on, Paul says this:

A wife is bound to her husband as long as he lives. If the husband dies, she is free to be married to whom she wishes, only in the Lord. (1 COR. 7:39)

Again, Paul here is talking about marriage under normal circumstances, as in a situation where a wife lives separate from her husband because she cannot tolerate his snoring or some other mild irritation! This verse does not apply to a violent marriage where a wife is being abused and harmed. (Remember, too, that Paul believed that everyone should remain unmarried, if at all possible, because the end of the world was coming. So his concern in his letters was not to give guidance to those seeking to remarry. Neither was his position on this question reflected in the Gospels.)

I was also abused by my father. I was an incest victim. How can I "honor" my father now?

I am certain that you learned in Sunday school to "honor your father and mother" as one of the Ten Commandments. You probably also learned that this meant that you had to obey your father no matter what he told you to do. This teaching made it easier for him to take advantage of you and sexually abuse you. You may have felt that you had no choice but to obey him.

The writer of Ephesians was concerned about this misuse of Scripture:

> Children, obey your parents in the Lord, for this is right. "Honor your father and mother" (this is the first commandment with a promise), "that it may be well with you and that you may live long on the earth." Fathers, do not provoke your children to anger, but bring them up in the discipline and instruction of the Lord. (EPH. 6:1–4)

The instructions here are to parents: do not provoke your children to anger. Nothing calls forth anger more intensely than the experience of abuse as a child at the hands of one's parent. Parents are cautioned and told to "bring them up in the discipline and instruction *of the Lord.*" This means that they should treat children as Jesus treated children. In no way can this be regarded as permission to sexually abuse a child.

Your father's abuse of you was wrong. He misused his power and his authority as your father. It was not your fault; it is his responsibility.

You may now have begun to feel angry, and you may decide to confront your father. It is an important step in your healing and also in offering him the opportunity to repent of his sin against you. Your anger can give you strength to write to him or to visit him and tell him how you feel about what he did. Try not to let your anger be vengeful; do not confront him in order to hurt him. Confront him because you need to break the silence that has surrounded your experience for years. It may be painful for him and for other family members to hear what you have to say, but this may be the only way that they can repent and return to God. What he did and the secret that has been protected all these years has separated him from you and from God.

If you do decide to talk to him or write him, remember that you deserve to have him acknowledge what he did, take responsibility, and say that he is sorry that he hurt you. Also keep in mind, however, that he may not do any of these things. He may still deny the events or blame you for them. In this case, you may feel once again betrayed and disappointed. Still, you will at least have tried. You will know that there is no relationship there with him. You will be able to let it go and mourn the loss. His refusal to acknowledge and to repent will bring your relationship to an end. But knowing this will be better than continuing a relationship based on a lie.

Now That I Am Doing Something About It . . .

You have made a decision to do whatever you can to protect yourself and your children from the violence in your home. It is a difficult decision because it means that you now face a lot of choices and don't really know what to expect or whom you can count on. You are probably getting conflicting advice from friends and family. You are looking for a way to understand your choices and to do God's will for you. Do not despair; there is a way through this.

I feel like God does not care. Nobody cares. I feel like God has abandoned me and does not answer my prayers.

It is certainly not unusual to feel this way, especially when many people have turned away from you when you have needed them. It is easy to conclude that God must have turned away, too. This is what the Psalmist felt:

My God, my God, why hast thou forsaken me?
   Why art thou so far from helping me, from
   the words of my groaning?
O God, I cry by day, but thou dost not
   answer; . . .

But I am scorned and despised by the people.
All who see me mock at me:
"[She] committed [her] cause to the Lord; let
   God deliver [her], let God rescue [her], for
   [she] delights in God" . . .
I am poured out like water, and all my bones
   are out of joint; my heart is like wax, it is
   melted within my breast; . . .
thou dost lay me in the dust of death. (PS.
   22:1–2, 6–8, 14, 15)

This may be how you feel at times. Yet, the
promise that we hear in scripture is that God will
be present to us when we are in greatest need.
Again, the Psalmist:

For [God] has not despised or abhorred the af-
fliction of the afflicted; and God has not hid
[God's] face from [her], but has heard, when
[she] cried to [God]. (PS. 22:24)

And in Psalm 118:5–7:

Out of my distress I called on the Lord; the
   Lord answered me and set me free.
With the Lord on my side I do not fear. What
   can [people] do to me?
The Lord is on my side to help me; I shall look
   in triumph on those who hate me.

God promises to be with us when we suffer and never to abandon us. This is sometimes hard to be certain of when things look most dismal for us.

You have probably heard the story about the woman who had always imagined that God walked with her in her life as if they were walking along the beach together. And she could look down as she walked and see two sets of footprints, hers and God's, so she knew that God was with her. During a particularly difficult time in her life, she again imagined herself walking along that beach, and she looked down and saw only one set of footprints. She despaired and decided that God had abandoned her and no longer walked with her. She felt overwhelmed and totally alone. However, she came through this difficult period, and when she looked back on it, she thought again about the footprints on the beach. Then she realized that the single set of footprints that she had seen were not hers, but God's, and that during this period of her life, God had picked her up and carried her along the beach.

Feelings of being abandoned are very real and frequently result from actually being abandoned by friends, family members, the church, or helpers when we are in crisis. But these experiences do not necessarily mean that God has also abandoned you. Watch and listen for God's presence regardless of what others do. God may be answering your prayers in unexpected ways and through unexpected people.

> *When people find out that I have been a battered woman, they avoid me. They see me as totally responsible for what happened; they don't trust me. I feel like a leper or something. Am I such a bad person?*

Some people may turn away from you just when you need them the most because they do not understand what you've been through. It may frighten them and make them uncomfortable, and so they "blame the victim" for having been abused. They may believe that if they avoid contact with you they will somehow protect themselves from the same kind of pain you have suffered. Their avoidance of you increases your isolation and makes you feel even worse about yourself.

As recounted in the Gospel of Luke (8:43–48), Jesus was walking in a crowd and suddenly felt someone touch him. He stopped and asked who it had been. His disciples, dismayed by his question, replied that in such a crowd it was impossible to know who had touched him. But Jesus persisted because he had felt someone touch him and his power go out to that person. Finally, a woman came forward, and although she was frightened, she admitted touching him and she declared that she had been healed. This was a woman who had had a flow of menstrual blood for twelve years. No one had been able to heal her illness. In those days, people believed that a menstruating woman was unclean and untouchable, so she had been ostracized by everyone who knew her for twelve years. Even though she had not caused the problem, she had felt bad about herself; she had been isolated and had had no friends.

But she had had courage. In spite of being "untouchable," she had reached out to touch Jesus in hopes of being healed. Through him she touched the holy spirit of God, which Jesus felt go out of him to her. When Jesus stopped and asked who had touched him, she was frightened because she had presumed to seek help for the illness that victimized her. But Jesus' reply was, "Daughter, your faith has made you well. Go in peace." She was rewarded for her faith and courage.

This story reminds us that even when everyone else turns away from us, God is still present. When no one else seems to understand the pain of being abused, God's healing spirit is with us. There is nothing shameful about being a victim of abuse, just as there is nothing shameful about being run over by a truck. Many people do not understand and do not want to see your pain because it makes them uncomfortable, just as the people did not want to acknowledge the suffering of the woman who was bleeding. Their avoidance of her only increased her suffering. But her courage and her faith helped her still to know God's presence in her life, which healed her illness and restored her to her community.

God does not turn away from us when we reach out to the spirit. God will send people to you who do understand your experience, people who may have had a similar experience in their lives and can appreciate the decisions you have made and the actions you have taken. Look for these people and walk with them.

I don't feel very trusting anymore, especially of men. I am really hesitant to start dating again. One man I dated for a while yelled at me during an argument, and I wouldn't see him again. Maybe I'm being silly or too particular.

No, you are taking care of yourself. You have some new expectations of a potential partner that are very reasonable; for example, you expect that you can have a relationship in which you are not afraid of being hit. It may take time to find a person whom you can trust and with whom you do not feel afraid. Trust your instincts. You deserve a relationship in which you feel safe and respected.

When Jesus gave instruction to his disciples, he said:

> Behold, I send you out as sheep in the midst of wolves; so be wise as serpents and innocent as doves. (MATT. 10:16)

Here the serpent is the one who is prudent, careful, and knows where it is going. The dove's innocence refers to simplicity and straightforwardness. So be wise and innocent, and remember that you are as a sheep among wolves. Listen to your own wisdom that you have gained from experience. Trust your expectations, and be straightforward in stating them. Look for another person who is also discerning, rather than someone who wants to control you, with whom to share your life.

I feel so angry for what he has done to me and my children. But Christian women aren't supposed to feel angry, are we?

When Jesus went to the temple in Jerusalem, he found it full of money changers and thieves. He was enraged, and he threw them all out and cleansed the temple (John 2:13–16). Jesus was angry that the holy place was being defiled and misused, and he did not hesitate to express his displeasure. Surely Jesus is even more angered when you or your children are harmed. Anger is the appropriate response to injustice and harm to others. It is all right to feel anger in such situations.

It is not all right to let your anger become violent, however. In Ephesians (4:26) we are instructed to

> Be angry but do not sin; do not let the sun go down on your anger.

In other words, your anger may be very legitimate, but do not do something sinful with it; for example, do not do something just to hurt your husband or just to seek revenge for what he has done to you. Do what you can to express your anger as soon as possible. You may be afraid to express it to him, so tell someone else. But do not deny that you feel angry about what he has done to you or your children. That is righteous anger, anger that is appropriate in response to what has been done to you.

I feel very bitter toward my husband, who abused me. The Bible says that I must forgive him. But I don't feel very forgiving. How can I forgive all that he did?

You may not be ready to forgive. You need not feel guilty for not being ready. Forgiveness is a process. You do not just wake up one morning, grit your teeth, and say, "Today I will forgive what he did to me." It also does not happen just because your pastor has urged you to forgive. If you are not ready, you will not really be forgiving.

In the Gospel of Luke (17:1–4), Jesus is instructing the disciples about forgiveness:

Take heed to yourselves; if your brother sins, rebuke him, and if he repents, forgive him; and if he sins against you seven times in the day, and turns to you seven times, and says, "I repent," you must forgive him.

Several important points are evident here. First, Jesus says to take care of yourself in all of this. Then, if someone abuses you (sins), rebuke him. In other words, somehow the abuser needs to hear that his behavior is wrong. This does not mean that you alone walk up to him and confront him. It more likely means that you ask others to help you in that, perhaps the police or the pastor or other family members. Whatever the case, someone needs to rebuke him. Then, Jesus says, *if* he repents, forgive him. This is a big *if*. Repentance here means more than remorse. Remorse is when he says, "I'm really sorry, honey; I didn't mean to hurt you. It will never happen again." Remorse usually gets expressed during the honeymoon or "making up" period of the battering cycle. The remorse may even be very genuine, but it does not mean that he will not hit again.

Repentance is much more significant. To repent, in both the Old and New Testaments, means to turn away from, to change, never to repeat again. True repentance on the part of the abuser means that he never hits again and that he learns to relate to other people in ways that are not controlling, demanding, and dominating. True repentance is not easy; it takes hard work for him to change his abusive way of relating to you. But this is what is expected. Only when you have seen true repentance (and over a period of time) can you consider forgiveness.

Sometimes a batterer will try to bargain with you: "If you forgive me, then I'll go get help for my problem." This is not the way it works. Repentance must come first; only then is true

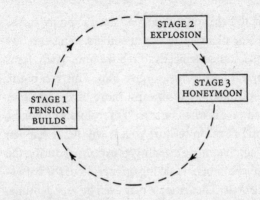

THE BATTERING CYCLE

forgiveness possible. Do not give in to his request for your forgiveness. Premature forgiveness does not help him or you.

The Battering Cycle was first described by Dr. Lenore Walker in *The Battered Woman* as a way of understanding the various stages of abusive incidents.

Stage 1: Tension builds in the batterer. He may be angry at his boss, irritated by heavy traffic on the freeway, anxious that he might not get a promotion at work, or disappointed that you prepared chicken instead of steak for dinner. Many abused women say that they can feel the tension building and feel like they are walking around on eggshells. This is the time that many women try very hard to do everything just right in order not to annoy him further. Unfortunately, this seldom works; regardless of how hard you try, he will hit when he is under stress.

Stage 2: The batterer explodes: an abusive incident. The batterer may hit, push, shove, yell, throw things, use a knife, gun, or other weapon. This is a very dangerous time; serious injury or death can easily result from the violence.

Stage 3: The batterer is remorseful, and the honeymoon follows. Many times the batterer will say he is sorry, he didn't mean to hurt you, he'll never do it again, and so forth following the violent episode. He will give you gifts and be very loving. This is a very difficult time because you will be tempted to believe his remorse and his promises in hopes that it will never happen again. Unfortunately, it will unless he gets some special help and comes to understand that he cannot continue to bring violence into his home. Tension starts to build again, and the cycle continues. The cycle can repeat itself once every six months or every hour, depending on the batterer.

What, then, is real forgiveness? Forgiveness does not mean "forgiving and forgetting," saying that everything is fine now, pardoning the abuse or ignoring it. Forgiveness means putting that experience in perspective, putting it behind you, and not allowing it to continue to victimize you. You can let go of it; you can remember it only when you need to. This is part of your healing of the pain of those experiences. Forgiveness is for you, not for the abuser. His repentance, not your forgiveness, is what will finally bring about his healing. Your forgiveness of him frees you from the memories of those experiences. This is what God wills for you so that you can get on with your life and share your gifts with others.

But even if your abusive partner never repents, you may at some point be ready to forgive. This will be made more possible if you have experienced support and affirmation from those around you. If your church and your pastor have heard your pain and supported you in getting away from the abuse, you may be ready to forgive. If the court has prosecuted your abuser and found him guilty, you may be ready to forgive. These are experiences of justice for you and may pave the way for you to heal and move on. But only you can know when you are ready. Then the Holy Spirit can give you the strength you need to forgive.

Instead of "forgive and forget," you need to "forgive and *remember*." Do not try to *not* think about your experience or else you will spend all of your time "not thinking" about it. Forgive (let it go) and remember what you have learned from the experience. Time and distance from the abuse itself will help you heal, and the memory of the abuse will not weigh you down. But it will remind you of important lessons that you are learning now about taking care of yourself.

> *If I leave him, I don't know how I will take care of myself and the kids. I don't have a job right now. How will I pay the bills or rent an apartment?*

These are certainly very real and immediate concerns that many abused women feel. This may be the first time that you have faced living alone and caring for your children. Jesus understood the anxiety we feel about these things and reassured us that we will be provided for:

> Therefore I tell you, do not be anxious about your life, what you shall eat or what you shall drink, nor about your body, what you shall put on. Is not life more than food, and the body

more than clothing? Look at the birds of the air: they neither sow nor reap nor gather into barns, and yet your heavenly [Creator] feeds them. Are you not of more value than they? . . . And why are you anxious about clothing? Consider the lilies of the field, how they grow; they neither toil nor spin; yet I tell you, even Solomon in all his glory was not arrayed like one of these. . . . Therefore do not be anxious, saying, "What shall we eat?" or "What shall we drink?" or "What shall we wear?" . . . Seek first [God's] kingdom and righteousness, and all these things shall be yours as well. Therefore do not be anxious about tomorrow, for tomorrow will be anxious for itself. Let the day's own trouble be sufficient for the day. (MATT. 6:25–26, 28–29, 31, 33–34)

God will provide for these immediate needs. God will use many people in your life and your community to assist you with these everyday necessities. Do not spend your energy being anxious, but look for the doors that God opens for you.

I feel that God has answered a lot of my prayers since I left my husband. Will God take care of me if I just lift all my worries up to God?

The Psalmist says:

But I call upon God; and the Lord will save me.
. . . Cast your burden on the Lord [who] will
sustain you. (PS. 55:16, 22)

God does promise to be present to us, especially in time of need. But our connection to the
holy spirit of God is not a passive relationship. In
other words, we cannot just sit down and do
nothing and expect God to take care of us. Jesus
said:

Ask, and it will be given you; seek, and you will
find; knock, and it will be opened to you. For
every one who asks receives, and [s]he who
seeks finds, and to [her] who knocks it will be
opened. (MATT. 7:7–8)

Ask, seek, knock. God expects us to do something. In the Book of Acts, we hear the story of
Peter's imprisonment by King Herod. He was
bound in chains and closely guarded by soldiers.
An angel appeared and woke Peter, saying:

"Get up quickly." And the chains fell off his
hands. And the angel said to him, "Dress yourself and put on your sandals." And he did so.

And he said to him, "Wrap your mantle around you and follow me." And he went out and followed him; he did not know that what was done by the angel was real, but thought he was seeing a vision. (ACTS 12:7–9)

They passed the guards, and when they came to the gate, it opened for them. They went out to the street, and then the angel left Peter. Then Peter realized that in fact God had sent the angel to rescue him from his bondage.

When the angel appeared to Peter, he told him what to do: these things were the things that Peter could do for himself. The angel took care of the things that Peter could not do for himself. God expects us to do whatever we are capable of for ourselves. When God answers, shows the way, and opens the door, then we have to walk through it. God will not pick us up and carry us through.

So if you have decided you do not want to live in an abusive relationship any longer, that you do not want your children to see their mother hurt by their father anymore, then you can ask God to show you the way out, to open the door. And when God shows you resources that can help you leave the abuse behind, you have to use those resources to take yourself and your children through that open door and away from the violence in your family. The resources are there: a friend, a pastor, a shelter or safe home, a phone number. God will give you the strength and courage to reach out for these supports and to walk through the door.

> *I just feel really up against a lot. I feel like the system isn't working. I'm trying to get a restraining order. I'm trying to get into a job-training program. And dealing with the welfare office is really hard. Sometimes I feel like I'm just beating my head against the wall.*

This is certainly an accurate sense of your situation when you keep running up against agencies or staff members who really are not very helpful or when the legal system does not take your complaint seriously. You get tired and frustrated and begin to feel like everything is working against you.

Jesus was concerned about this sense of being overwhelmed and told a parable to the effect that we ought always to pray and not lose heart. He said,

> In a certain city there was a judge who neither feared God nor regarded [persons]; and there

was a widow in that city who kept coming to him and saying, "Vindicate me against my adversary." For a while he refused; but afterward he said to himself, "Though I neither fear God nor regard [persons], yet because this widow bothers me, I will vindicate her, or she will wear me out by her continual coming." And the Lord said, "Hear what the unrighteous judge says. And will not God vindicate [the] elect, who cry to [God] day and night? Will [God] delay long over them? I tell you, [God] will vindicate them speedily. Nevertheless, when the Son of [humanity] comes, will he find faith on earth?" (LUKE 18:1–8)

There are two purposes to Jesus' story. First, he shows us a widow (a woman in a situation at that time with little support from the community) who takes her request for justice to the system. Even though the system does not care about her, it finally gives her what she requests just to be rid of her. Her persistence pays off. Second, Jesus puts her situation in a larger context: if even an uncaring system finally gives her what she deserves, then surely God will give her even more; God will truly give her justice. But even so, when Jesus comes to us, will he find us keeping faith?

Luke says in the introduction to this parable that we "ought always to pray and not lose heart." Prayer and persistence will help us to keep faith with one another, will help us to be there for each other when we are in need, to lift and carry each other's burdens a ways, to stand by, sometimes to speak for, or to just sit with and listen.

A Final Word

A woman who was raped when she was nineteen realized several years later when she thought back to that experience how her prayer life had changed. She recalled that as a teenager, she had often prayed the way she was taught in Sunday school: "O God, please take care of me." Now, as an adult woman, she had survived a sexual assault and begun to feel healed of that pain. She realized that she now prayed, "O God, help me to remember what I have learned."

This change in her prayer life signified a change in her. In the trauma of the rape her faith had grown from a passive dependence on God to "protect" her to a realization of the need for her active self-care based on what she learned in her own experience. Her relationship with God was maturing and gave her the strength to care for herself.

You have had painful experiences. Perhaps you have been abandoned, exiled from your church or community, blamed for your own victimization, not been believed. But you are a strong woman. You have survived, you have cared for your children and your home, you have served in your church, you have worked at your job. You have kept body and soul together; you have kept the faith.

There are many who walk with you. And there are many others who need you to walk with them. Pray that God will help you to remember what you have learned. And share what you know with other women who may be facing the same circumstance as you.

❧ *Prayers and Meditations*

Prayers
and Meditations

The following prayers, scriptural passages, and short quotations are provided for your prayer and meditation. Write some of your own prayers or meditations. Find a quiet time and place each day for yourself. Do not hesitate to share your true feelings with God; God can handle them and will not turn away from you.

❧

Do you not know that you are God's temple and that God's Spirit dwells in you? If any one destroys God's temple, God will destroy him. For God's temple is holy, and that temple you are. (1 COR. 3:16–17)

❧

By His Wounds you have been Healed. (1 PET. 2:24)

❧

In a Toronto church, a sculpture depicting a woman, arms outstretched as if crucified, was hung below the cross in the chancel. The reaction of church members and the public was strong: some were outraged by it, and others felt it a powerful symbol through which they came to experience the crucifixion of Jesus in a new way. "By His Wounds You Have Been Healed" appeared in *No Longer Strangers* (1983).

O God,
through the image of a woman
crucified on the cross
I understand at last.

For over half of my life
I have been ashamed
of the scars I bear.
These scars tell an ugly story,
a common story,
about a girl who is the victim
when a man acts out his fantasies.

In the warmth, peace and sunlight of your
   presence
I was able to uncurl the tightly clenched fists.
For the first time
I felt your suffering presence with me

in that event.
I have known you as a vulnerable baby,
as a brother, and as a father.
Now I know you as a woman.
You were there with me
as the violated girl
caught in helpless suffering.

The chains of shame and fear
no longer bind my heart and body.
A slow fire of compassion and forgiveness
is kindled.
My tears fall now
For man as well as woman.

You, God,
can make our violated bodies
vessels of love and comfort
to such a desperate man.
I am honoured
to carry this womanly power
within my body and soul.

You were not ashamed of your wounds.
You showed them to Thomas
as marks of your ordeal and death.
I will no longer hide these wounds of mine.
I will bear them gracefully.
They tell a resurrection story.

❧

This prayer was prepared by Ruth C. Duck
and is taken from *Bread for the Journey* (1981).

God of endless possibility, we confess that we
do not always perceive the opportunities you
place before us. Caught up in our own hopes,
plans, and fantasies, and crushed when they dis-
appoint us, we are slow to see the open path-
ways you set before us. Open our eyes, that we
may accept the new life you offer us, and thus
show forth the resurrection of Jesus Christ.
Amen.

❧

Do not neglect to show hospitality to strangers,
for thereby some have entertained angels un-
awares. Remember those who are in prison, as
though in prison with them; and those who are
ill-treated, since you also are in the body. Let
marriage be held in honor among all, and let the
marriage bed be undefiled; for God will judge
the immoral and adulterous. Keep your life free
from love of money, and be content with what
you have; for [God] has said, "I will never fail
you nor forsake you." Hence we can confidently

say, "The Lord is my helper, I will not be afraid;
what can man do to me?" (HEB. 13:2–6)

❧

Ntozake Shange is a poet and writer who
wrote *for colored girls who have considered sui-
cide/when the rainbow is enuf.* It is a choreopoem,
a long poem performed on stage with a number
of different black women speaking portions of
the poem, and is written in dialect. One section of
the poem is called "sorry" (1980) and is excerpted
here. The women are speaking about their husbands and boyfriends being sorry for hurting
them. Think about the times you have been hurt
and then heard the words "I'm sorry, honey."

"i'm only human, and inadequacy is what
   makes us human, & if we
was perfect we wdnt have nothin to strive for,
   so you might as
well go on and forgive me pretty baby, cause
   i'm sorry"
"shut up bitch, i told you i waz sorry"
no this one is it, "i do you like i do cause i thot
   ya could
take it, now i'm sorry"

one thing i dont need
is any more apologies
i got sorry greetin me at my front door
you can keep yrs
i dont know what to do wit em
they dont open doors
or bring the sun back
they dont make me happy
or get a mornin paper
didnt nobody stop usin my tears to wash cars
cuz a sorry

i am simply tired
of collectin
   "i didnt know
   i was so important to you"
i'm gonna haveta throw some away
i cant get to the clothes in my closet
for alla the sorries
i'm gonna tack a sign to my door
leave a message by the phone
   "if you called
   to say yr sorry
   call somebody
   else
   i dont use em anymore"

you were always inconsistent
doin somethin & then bein sorry
beatin my heart to death
talkin bout you sorry

I loved you on purpose
i was open on purpose
i still crave vulnerability & close talk
& i'm not even sorry bout you being sorry

you can carry all the guilt & grime ya wanna
just dont give it to me
i cant use another sorry
next time
you should admit
you're mean/low-down/triflin/& no count
   straight out
steada bein sorry alla the time
enjoy bein yourself

❧

Deliver me, O Lord, from evil men; preserve
   me from violent men,
who plan evil things in their heart, and stir up
   wars continually.
They make their tongue sharp as a serpent's,
   and under their lips is the poison of vipers.

Guard me, O Lord, from the hands of the
wicked; preserve me from violent men, who
have planned to trip up my feet.

Arrogant men have hidden a trap for me, and
with cords they have spread a net, by the
wayside they have set snares for me.

I say to the Lord, Thou art my God; give ear to
the voice of my supplications, O Lord!

O Lord, my Lord, my strong deliverer, thou has
covered my head in the day of battle.

Grant not, O Lord, the desires of the wicked;
do not further his evil plot!

Those who surround me lift up their head, let
the mischief of their lips overwhelm them!

Let burning coals fall upon them! Let them be
cast into pits, no more to rise!

Let not the slanderer be established in the land;
let evil hunt down the violent man speedily!

I know that the Lord maintains the cause of the
afflicted, and executes justice for the needy.

Surely the righteous shall give thanks to thy
name; the upright shall dwell in thy presence.
(PS. 140)

❧

This prayer was prepared by Ruth C. Duck
and is taken from *Bread for the Journey* (1981).

O God, in mystery and silence you are present in our lives, bringing new life out of destruction, hope out of despair, growth out of difficulty. We thank you that you do not leave us alone but labor to make us whole. Help us to perceive your unseen hand in the unfolding of our lives, and to attend to the gentle guidance of your Spirit, that we may know the joy you give your people. Amen.

❧

The following selection is "Meditation on Luke 1" by Dorothee Sölle, from *Revolutionary Patience* (1977). Sölle is a German Protestant theologian now teaching in the United States. Her poem paraphrases the story of God's coming to Mary to tell her that she would give birth to Jesus.

It is written that mary said
my soul doth magnify the lord
and my spirit hath rejoiced in god my savior
for he hath regarded the low estate of his
  handmaiden
for behold from henceforth
all generations shall call me blessed

Today we express that differently
my soul sees the land of freedom

my spirit will leave anxiety behind
the empty faces of women will be filled with
   life
we will become human beings
long awaited by the generations sacrificed
   before us

It is written that mary said
for he that is mighty hath done to me great
   things
and holy is his name
and his mercy is on them that fear him
from generation to generation

Today we express that differently
the great change that is taking place in us and
   through us
will reach all—or it will not take place
charity will come about when the oppressed
can give up their wasted lives
and learn to live themselves

It is written that mary said
he hath shewed strength with his arm
he hath scattered the proud
he hath put down the mighty from their seats
and exalted them of low degree

Today we express that differently
we shall dispossess our owners and we shall
   laugh
at those who claim to understand feminine
   nature
the rule of males over females will end
objects will become subjects
they will achieve their own better right

It is written that mary said
he hath filled the hungry with good things
and the rich he hath sent empty away
he hath holpen his servant israel
in remembrance of his mercy

Today we express that differently
women will go to the moon and sit in
   parliaments
their desire for self-determination will be
   fulfilled
the craving for power will go unheeded
their fears will be unnecessary
and exploitation will come to an end

❧

For thou hast been a stronghold to the poor,
a stronghold to the needy in [her] distress, a

shelter from the storm and a shade from the
heat; for the blast of the ruthless is like a storm
against a wall, like heat in a dry place. Thou dost
subdue the noise of the aliens; as heat by the
shade of a cloud, so the song of the ruthless is
stilled. (ISA. 25:4–5)

❧

The Lord is my light and my salvation: whom
    shall I fear? The Lord is the stronghold of my
    life; of whom shall I be afraid? . . .
One thing I have asked of the Lord, that will I
    seek after; that I may dwell in the house of the
    Lord all the days of my life, to behold the
    beauty of the Lord, and to inquire in [God's]
    temple.
For [God] will hide me in [a] shelter in the day
    of trouble; [God] will conceal me under the
    cover of [God's] tent, [God] will set me high
    upon a rock. . . .
Turn not thy servant away in anger, thou who
    hast been my help. Cast me not off, forsake
    me not, O God of my salvation!
For my father and my mother have forsaken
    me, but the Lord will take me up.
Teach me thy way, O Lord; and lead me on a
    level path because of my enemies.

Give me not up to the will of my adversaries;
   for false witnesses have risen against me, and
   they breathe out violence.
I believe that I shall see the goodness of the
   Lord in the land of the living!
Wait for the Lord; be strong, and let your heart
   take courage; yea, wait for the Lord! (PS. 27:1,
   4–5, 9–14)

❧

This prayer was prepared by Ruth C. Duck
and is taken from *Bread for the Journey* (1981).

God of tenderness, we thank you that you care
for us individually and intimately. We thank
you that you know us through and through and
yet love us. Jesus said that the hairs of our heads
are numbered and that you care even for the
sparrows. As you are aware of our needs, so
awaken us to the needs of others, that we may
respond in concern. Amen.

❧

"Let Me Pass the Day in Peace," from the Boran
of Kenya, is taken from *No Longer Strangers* (1983).

O God, you have let me pass the day in peace,
Let me pass the night in peace.

O Lord, you have no Lord.
There is no strength but in you.
There is no unity but in your house.
Under your hand I pass the night.
You are my mother and my father.
You are my home. Amen.

❧

The following selection is "Psalm," by Julia Emily Louisa Peebles, from *Woman-soul Flowing* (1978).

We trust that beyond the absence: there is a presence.
That beyond the pain: there can be healing.
That beyond the brokenness: there can be wholeness.
That beyond the anger: there may be peace.
That beyond the hurting: there may be forgiveness.
That beyond the silence: there may be the word.
That through the word: there may be understanding.
That through understanding: there is love.

❧

Christmas is not an easy time for a Christian abused woman. You may be in a shelter: you may be alone. Use this short Christmas Eve service to reflect on the meaning for you of Jesus' coming into the world. The service was prepared as an Advent service of worship by Reverend Carrie Doehring and is entitled "The Darkness of Violence, the Light of God's Healing Presence" (from *Glad Tidings*, Vol. 61, No. 10, December 1985).

Call to Worship: We gather together, aware of the darkness around us. The darkness is violence, and the fear, distrust and betrayal that comes from violence. The darkness may be part of our home, or of our neighbour's home. The darkness is part of our society, in media images and in pornography. The darkness is part of our world, when nation mistrusts nation. We gather together, aware of the darkness around us. We remember the people, long ago, who walked in darkness. We remember the darkness of Bethlehem.

Hymn: "Christ Is the World's True Light" or "Come, Thou Long-expected Jesus"

Prayer of Confession: O God of Truth, we recognize that violence is part of our life, and we name this violence as sin. We confess that for a long time we have called this violence by names we could tolerate. We have called physical abuse, discipline. We have called violence, a family fight. We have called isolation, a need for privacy.

O God of Light, we acknowledge that family violence has been a secret among us for a long time. We have helped to keep this secret. We confess that we shut our eyes to the bruises. We have shut our ears to the cries of fear and pain. We name this silence and apathy as sin.

O God of Light and Peace, there is darkness in our homes, and in our world. We claim our responsibility for allowing this darkness to continue. We seek your peace and healing for our homes and for the world.

Assurance of Pardon: Within us and among us, God's forgiveness is born whenever we acknowledge our sin and truly repent. Let us begin and continue the long process of change within ourselves, our community, and the world, so that the darkness of violence is no longer tolerated.

Hymn: "O Little Town of Bethlehem"

Scripture: (Listen to these readings with the ears of a child or person—especially a woman—who is living with violence at home.)

Psalm 55:1–15, 20–21
Jeremiah 31:7–13
John 1:1–5
1 John 1:5–7a

Hymn: "The Race That Long in Darkness"

A Prayer of Dedication (said in unison): We offer ourselves to you, O God our Creator. We offer our hands. Use healing touch to comfort sisters and children who are afraid. We offer our eyes and ears. May we see and hear the signs and stories of violence, so that sisters and children have someone with them in their pain and confusion. We offer our hearts and our tears as their hurt and sorrow echo within us. We offer our own stories of violence. May we be healed as we embrace each other. We offer our anger. Make it a passion for justice. We offer all our skills. Use our gifts to end violence. We offer our faith, our hope, our love. May our encounters with violence bring us closer to you and each other.

Hymn: "It Came upon a Midnight Clear"

The Blessing: May the light of God shine in our darkness. May the peace of God dwell in our homes. May the justice of God rule in our community. May the healing of God mend our brokenness. May the blessing of God, our Creator, Redeemer and Sustainer dwell within us and among us, now and forever. Amen.

Suggestions for the Abused Woman

Suggestions for the Abused Woman

How to Deal with Your Pastor

If you have not yet talked with your pastor or priest about the abuse you have experienced, there is probably a good reason. You probably intuitively sense that he or she will not be helpful to you. This may be because you have never heard your clergyperson mention anything about wife abuse. Or it may be because you have heard something mentioned that made it clear that your experience would not be understood or believed. Trust your feelings about this. Do not go to this person unless you feel safe and assured that your clergyperson will listen, understand, and believe you. If you are simply unsure, take someone with you—preferably a shelter counselor or support group leader who can support you and help your pastor or priest learn about your situation. If you have already gone to your pastor or priest, I hope you found sensitivity and support. Share this book with him or her, and ask for any further help you feel you need.

If you found your pastor or priest unhelpful, if you were not believed or you were counseled to

- ❧ submit to your husband
- ❧ pray harder
- ❧ try to get your husband to church
- ❧ be a better Christian wife
- ❧ lift up the abuse to the Lord
- ❧ forgive your abuser and take him back

without dealing with the battering and abuse, then that person does not understand what you have been through. He or she has no comprehension of your experience and no information about wife abuse. At this point this person will not be a helpful resource to you.

Remember that most ministers have not received any training to prepare them to understand your abuse. Although they may care deeply about you and want to help, their lack of knowledge and skill will prevent them from being the support that you need. Do not feel guilty about choosing not to discuss your abuse further with your minister at this time. God will provide other pastors or priests who may be more knowledgeable and prepared to help.

How to Deal with a Shelter Counselor

If you have considered going to a shelter or have contacted a crisis line, you may have felt hesitant for fear that the counselor would not understand your Christian beliefs. Most shelters are not specifically Christian although many shelters rely on Christians in many different roles to provide their services. Do not assume that you will not find a Christian staff person or volunteer when you call a shelter or crisis line—you may be surprised.

But you may also find someone who does not understand your beliefs or who is not currently an active Christian. Do not assume because of this that she cannot be of help to you. God works in mysterious ways and may send you an angel disguised as a shelter counselor. She has information you need; she has resources you need; she believes you and cares what happens to you. Give her a chance to help.

If she seems uncomfortable when you talk about your religious concerns, it is probably because she does not understand some aspects of the Christian faith or the significance it has for you. She may also be concerned that you may be trapped by some of the distortions of Christian teaching and not be aware of the help that your faith can be to you in this crisis.

How to Deal with Other Women in the Shelter or Support Group

If you go to a shelter or support group, you will find women just like you—they have all been through abuse much like yours. But you will also find that there are women who come from backgrounds, races, and religious groups different from yours. Try to respect these differences. What is helping you right now in dealing with the abuse may not be helpful for them. Your faith may be the cornerstone of your efforts to end the abuse in your life and protect your children. But their church may have been hurtful to them, and they may need some space to recover and search out their faith in a new way. Pray for them; give them room to hear God's voice in their way and their time; do not impose your way on them.

❧ *Suggestions*
for Clergy and
Laypersons

Suggestions for Clergy and Laypersons

How to Be Helpful to the Christian Battered Woman

The Bible has often been misinterpreted and misused in response to the Christian battered woman by those who have wanted to help her. This has been sometimes due to ignorance, sometimes due to denial of the seriousness of wife abuse, sometimes due to a desire to control the battered woman and limit her options.

Particularly within Christian churches, there is a tendency to focus the discussion about wife abuse on the question of how to keep the family together at any cost. Hence, at times the well-intended advice of a pastor or church friend has discouraged the battered woman from leaving an abusive situation, in order to "keep the family together." Tragically, this advice does nothing to stop the abuse and may in fact endanger the battered woman and her children and ultimately destroy the family.

As one called upon to help a Christian battered woman, it is important that you understand several things about what she has been experiencing.

- ❧ The abuse she has experienced has probably included physical beating, threat of weapon use or actual use of weapons, marital rape, psychological coercion and control (much like that experienced by a prisoner of war), and destruction of her property (clothes, car, china, and so on) or pets.

- ❧ Her children may have experienced physical or sexual abuse by their father. Their witnessing of their mother being abused by their father has already given them a distorted picture of marriage and family life as being a place of fear and pain.

- ❧ She has probably endured this abuse for months or years. She has remained in a situation that is destructive to her and her children because she loves her husband, wants to keep her family intact, perhaps needs his economic support, believes she can change him, has been told by the church to stay, and is afraid that his violence toward her will increase if she leaves.

❖ She cannot change his abuse toward her; she cannot stop his violence by changing her behavior. She has already tried that in every way she can think of. She does not "provoke" or "enjoy" his abuse. He needs expert help with his problem. The fact is that he has learned to hit and control others when he is under stress in his life. By relating to his family in this way, he is destroying it.

❖ Unless he works to stop his violence, he could very well end up killing her and his children. Even if his violence never reaches this extreme, he is breaking apart his marriage and his family by his violence.

❖ Right now what she needs is a safe place where she need not be afraid of his finding her in order to recover from the devastation of this chronic abuse. She needs someone who believes her story of what she has experienced and who can support her in protecting herself and her children.

There are three goals that you should keep in mind as you respond to her.

1. *Protect the victim (and children) from further abuse.* This may mean calling the police to an emergency situation, referring the woman and her children to a shelter or safe home, or helping her go out of state to stay with a relative. The point is that she needs immediate safety, and we need to find a way to provide that as best we can.

2. *Stop the abuser's violence.* This may also mean calling the police to make an arrest, referring the abuser to a treatment program, or simply confronting him using our pastoral authority and telling him that his violence has to stop. We should not try to accomplish this alone. We need to call on the resources of the community to help him.

3. *Restore the marriage and family if possible, or mourn its loss.*

Before goal number 3 can be accomplished, the first two goals must be achieved. This means that in order for you to assist the Christian battered woman in restoring her marriage, you must first of all help her protect herself and ensure that the abuser has stopped battering. If you try to begin with goal number 3, avoiding the first two, you will fail.

It is possible that even when goals number 1 and 2 are accomplished, the marriage cannot be restored. The damage may be too severe for the woman to ever recover a sense of trust and safety. Or if the abuser refuses to repent and to seek help for his problem, there is no hope for restoration. In these cases, the only option is to mourn the loss of this relationship and deal openly and supportively with the reality of a broken marriage leading to divorce.

This is sometimes difficult for a Christian pastor who sees a high priority in avoiding divorce at all costs. The reality is that the abuser's violence has already destroyed this marriage, and its only hope for restoration is if the abuser stops abusing. This is also the only hope for the abuser's salvation: he must be called to repentance, and his repentance can only be made real in his efforts never to bring violence into his home again.

In order to work on goals number 1 and 2, it is often necessary for the battered woman to temporarily leave the home and go to a shelter or safe home or to stay with friends or family. She may need your support and encouragement to take this step. Refer her to local resources like a shelter or crisis line. They are skilled in assisting battered women. Work with them in order to minister effectively to her needs.

Do not contact the abuser or disclose any information to him about her discussions with you. You could endanger her life. Do not suggest couples counseling. It will not work to stop the abuser's violence. It may be useful later on after the abuser has received the treatment he needs. Do not discourage her from using the legal system if she so chooses. Arrest and conviction are a very effective way to call the abuser to account and to get him started on the road to repentance. In most communities he will be sentenced to a treatment program, not to jail. This is the help he needs.

You can be a valuable help to the Christian battered woman who seeks you out. You can provide her with information about available community resources; you can reassure her and discuss with her possible religious questions she is likely to have; you can pray with her and be present to her pain; you can share this book with her.

Suggested Readings

Suggested Readings

Bass, Ellen, ed. *I Never Told Anyone: A Collection of Writings by Women Survivors of Sexual Child Abuse.* New York: Harper & Row, 1983. Honest and straightforward.

Bussert, Joy M. K. *Battered Women.* New York: Division for Mission in North America, Lutheran Church in America, 1986. Subtitled "From a Theology of Suffering to an Ethic of Empowerment," this book is a most welcome addition to the field from the perspective of a Christian pastor. It is the first effort to deal with the theological roots not only of sexism but of violence and punishment within marriage.

Butler, Sandra. *Conspiracy of Silence.* San Francisco: Volcano Press, 1978. An early but still very helpful discussion of incest that incorporates powerful stories from survivors.

Byerly, Carolyn. *The Mother's Book.* Dubuque, IA: Kendall-Hunt, 1985. A handbook for nonoffending mothers of incest victims that provides valuable information about the aftermath of disclosure. Available from the Washington State

Coalition of Sexual Assault Programs, 110 East 5th St., #214, Olympia, WA 98501.

Child Sexual Abuse in Native American Communities. National American Indian Court Judges Association. A valuable booklet providing basic information for Native American communities. Available from the National Indian Law Library, 1506 Broadway, Butler, CO 80302.

Duck, Ruth C., ed. *Bread for the Journey.* New York: Pilgrim Press, 1981.

Fortune, Marie M. *Sexual Violence—The Unmentionable Sin.* New York: Pilgrim Press, 1983. An ethical and pastoral perspective from a Christian minister that deals with rape and child sexual abuse.

Gjerding, Iben and Katherine Kinnamon. *No Longer Strangers,* Geneva, Switzerland: World Council of Churches, 1983.

He Told Me Not to Tell. King County Rape Relief. Excellent parents' guide to talking with children. Available from King County Rape Relief, 305 South 43rd, Renton, WA 98055.

Hindman, Jan. *A Very Touching Book.* Durkee, OR: McClure Hindman Books, 1983. Delightfully illustrated and carefully conveyed information children need; includes discussion of incest. Ages 5–12.

Martin, Del. *Battered Wives.* San Francisco: Volcano Press, 1981. This edition is a revised edition of the first book in the United States to bring this problem into the open. A classic.

Shange, Ntozake. *for colored girls who have considered suicide/when the rainbow is enuf.* New York: Bantam, 1980.

Sölle, Dorothee. *Revolutionary Patience.* Maryknoll, NY: Orbis Books, 1977.

Wachter, Oralee. *No More Secrets for Me.* New York: Little-Brown, 1983. Stories about children approached sexually by adults and how they solved their problems. Accurate information. Ages 6–10.

Williams, Joy. *Red Flag, Green Flag.* Rape and Abuse Center of Fargo-Moorhead, 1980. Available from P.O. Box 2984, Fargo, ND 58108. Good and bad touch simply explained for ages 2–6. Available in Spanish.

Woman-soul Flowing. Chicago: Ecumenical Women's Center, 1978.

Acknowledgments

Grateful acknowledgment is made for use of the following: "By His Wounds You Have Been Healed" and "Let Me Pass the Day in Peace" from *No Longer Strangers*, edited by Iben Gjerding and Katherine Kinnamon. Copyright © 1983 by WCC, LWF, WSCF, WYWCS, Geneva, Switzerland. Used by permission. From *Bread for the Journey: Resources for Worship*, by Ruth C. Duck. Copyright © 1981 The Pilgrim Press. Used by permission. From *for colored girls who have considered suicide/when the rainbow is enuf*, by Ntozake Shange. Copyright © 1975, 1976, 1977 by Ntozake Shange. Used by permission of Macmillan Publishing Company. "Meditation on Luke 1" from *Revolutionary Patience*, by Dorothee Sölle. Copyright © 1974 by Dorothee Sölle. Used by permission of Orbis Books. "Psalm" from *Woman-soul Flowing*, by Julia Emily Louisa Peebles. Copyright © 1978. Used by permission of